Thank you for c| our Coloring Book!

In cooperation with KIWI Publishing

Our books are designed with love and care for for your little one.

Please leave a review on Amazon. It is very much appreciated! It helps us develop fun and educational books for your child.

We also included a FREE Coloring Book for your kid! - 100 Pages to color! Scan the QR code below!

Scan the simple Qr code below and it will take you directly to the review page on Amazon!

Leave a Review

My FREE Coloring Book

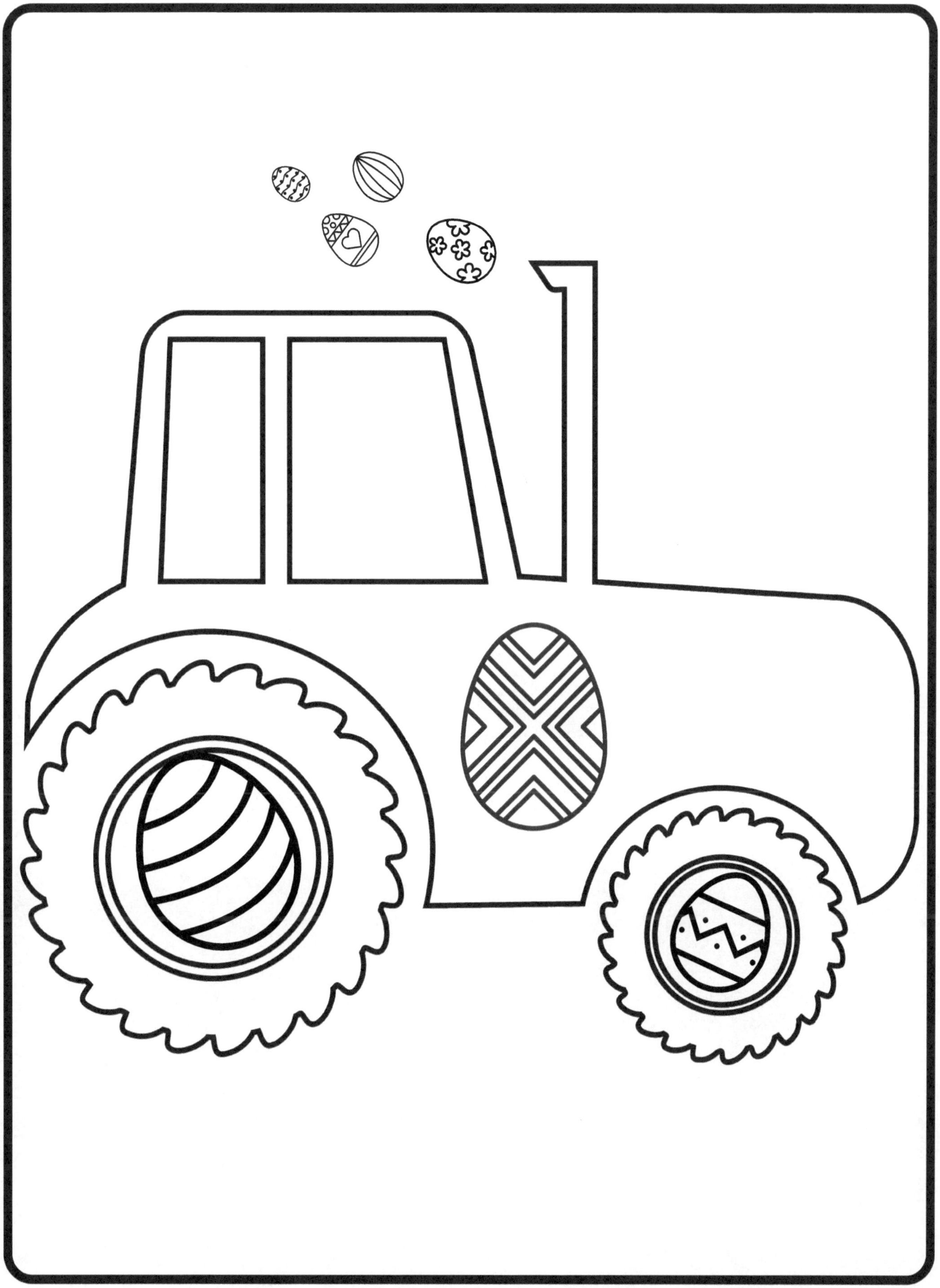

DIG EASTER

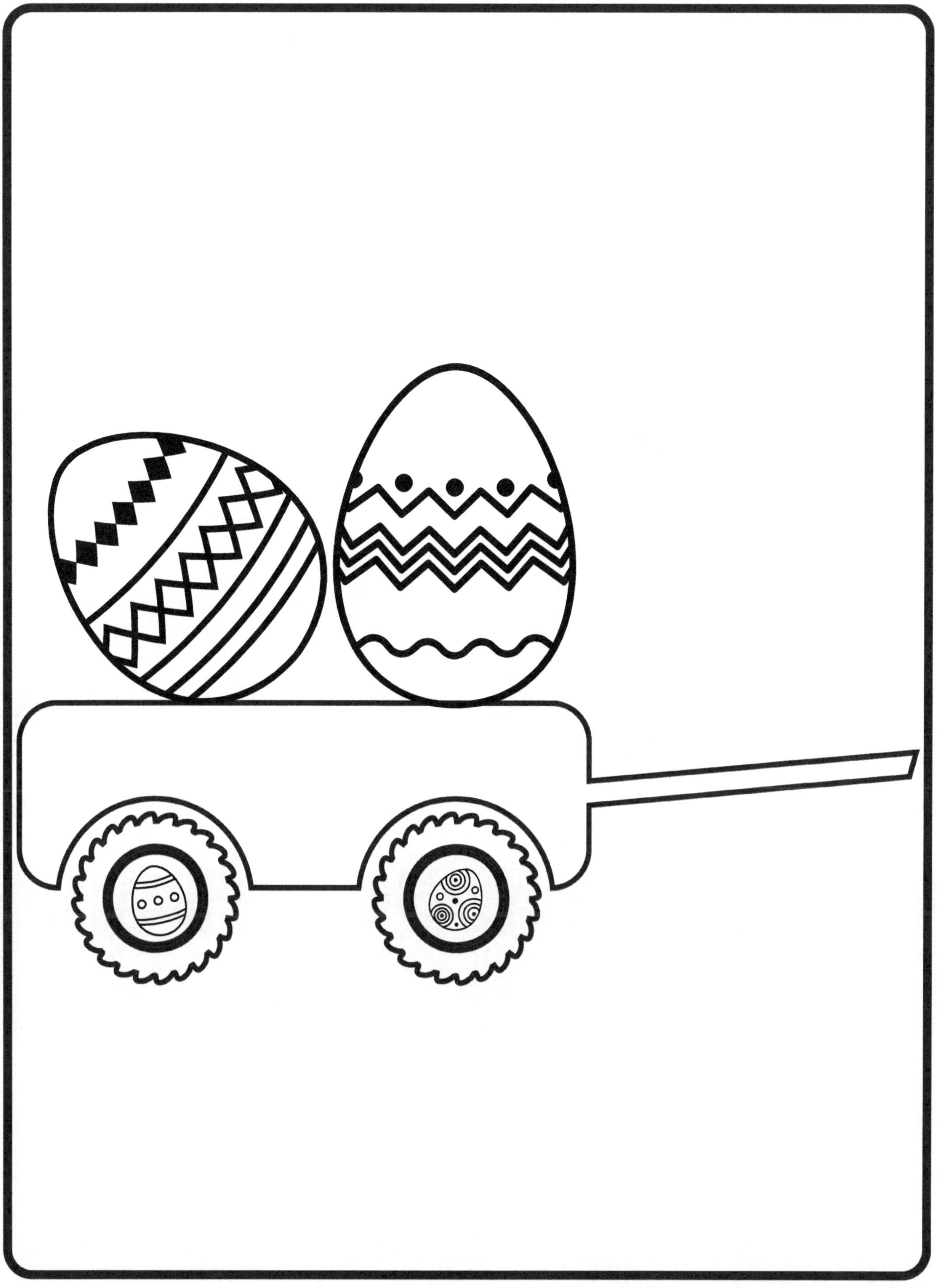

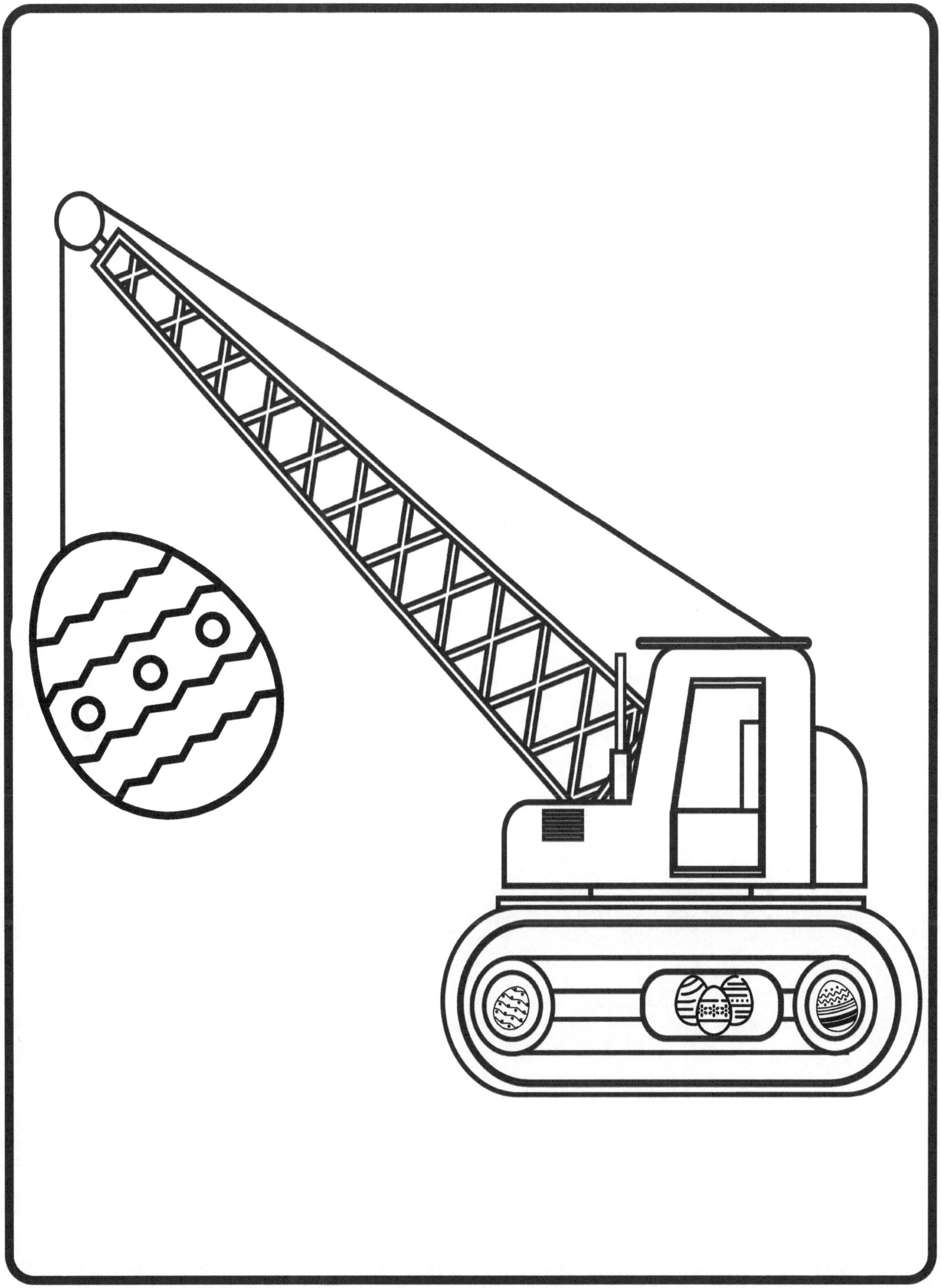

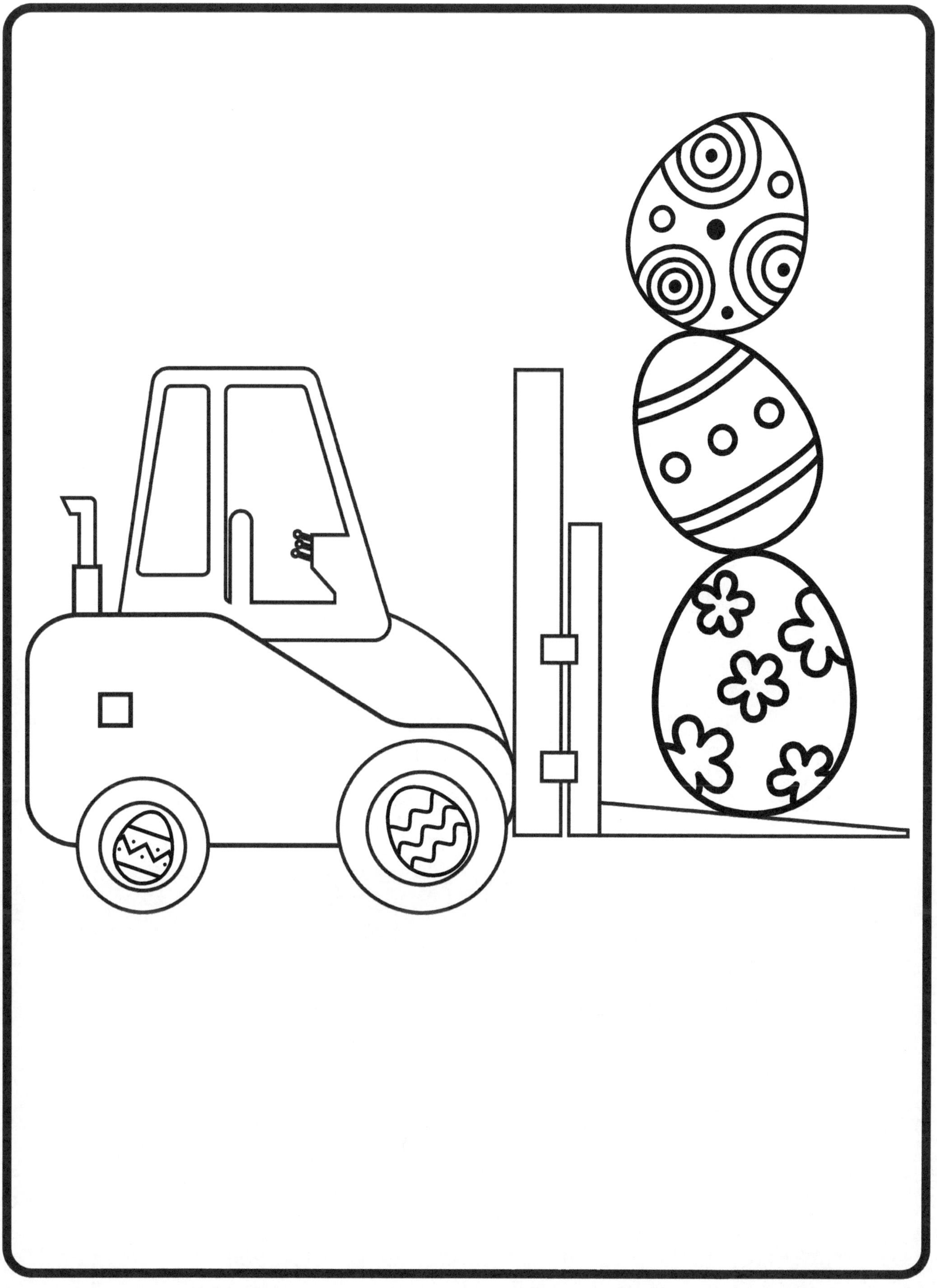

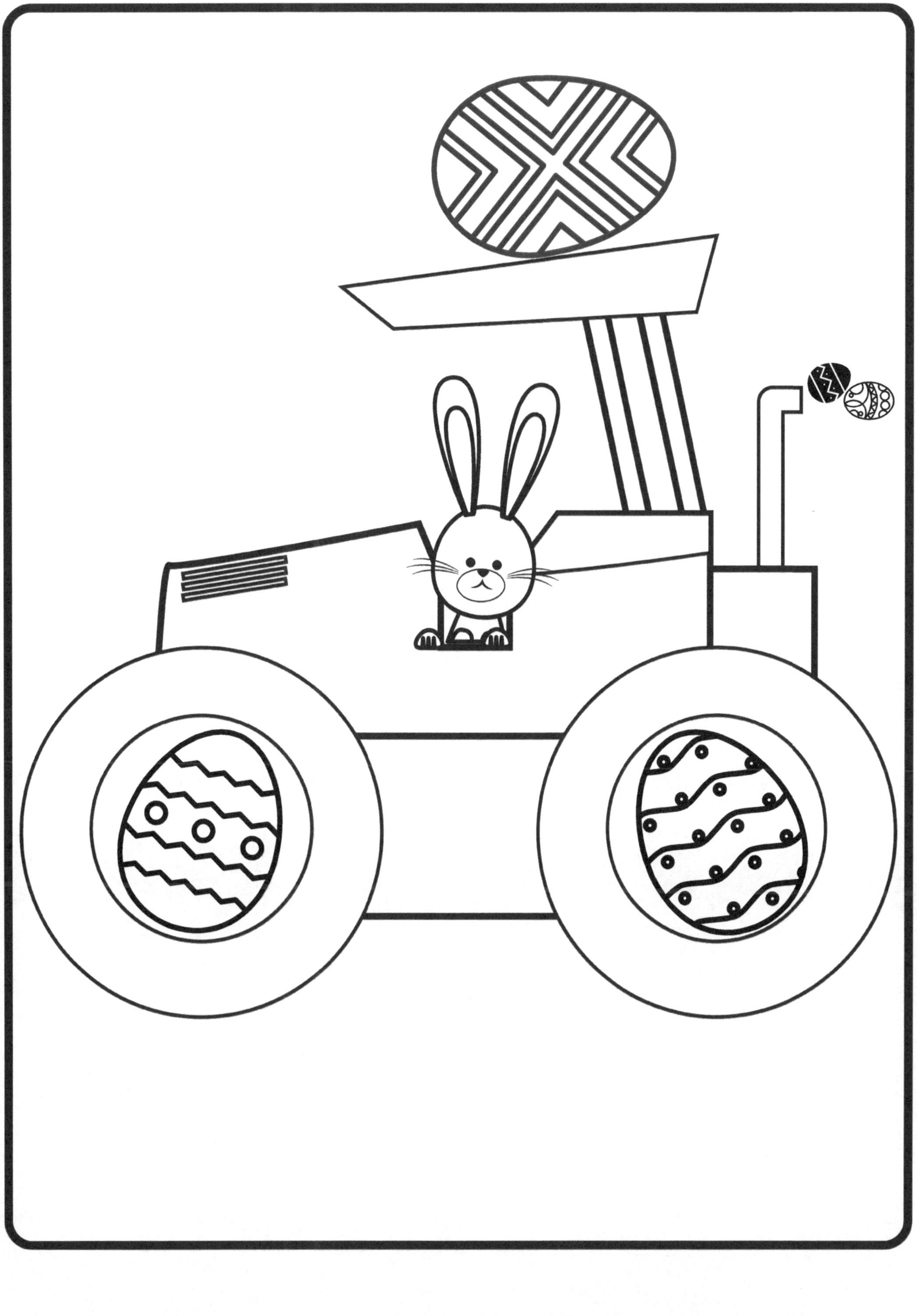

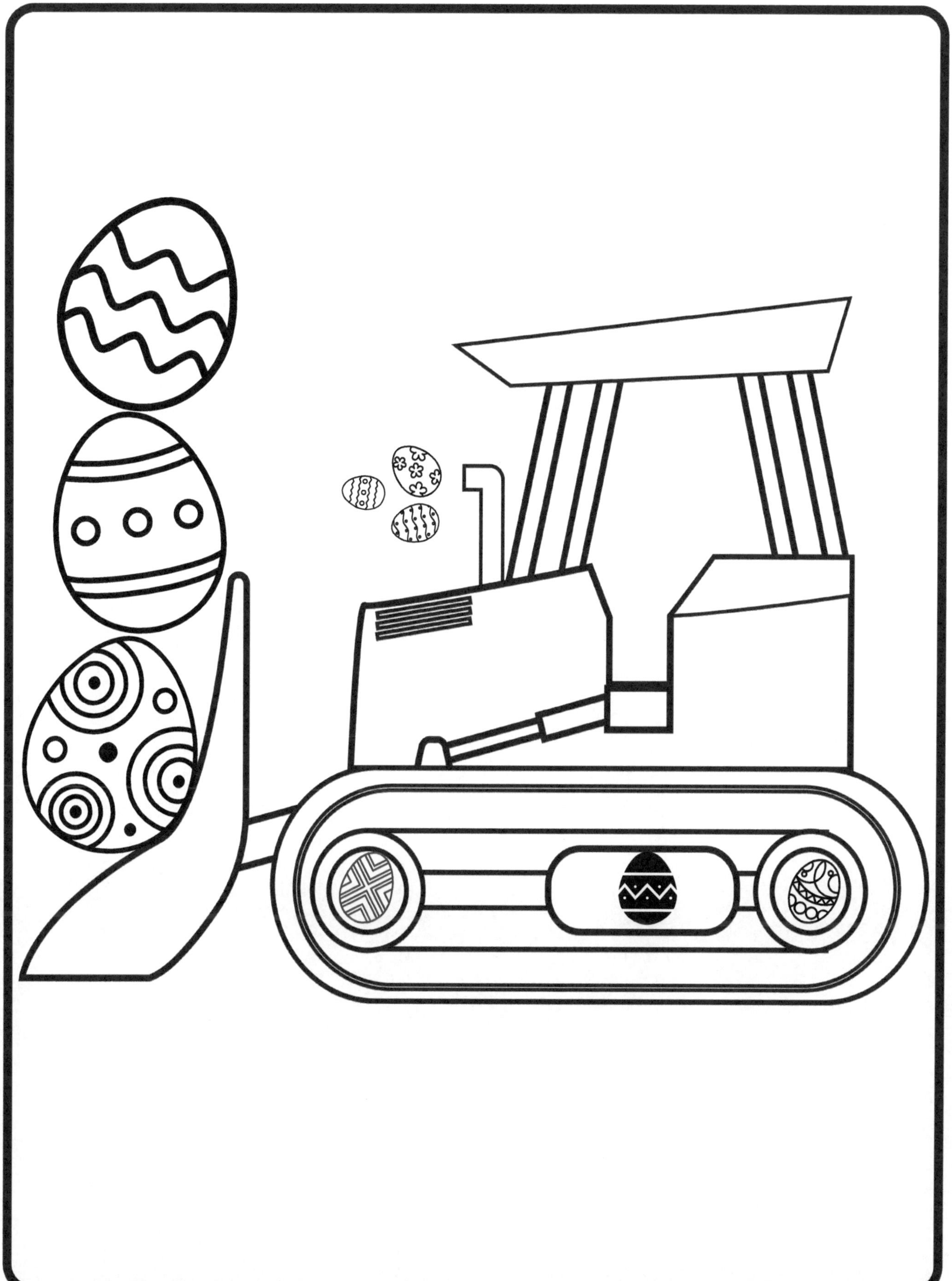

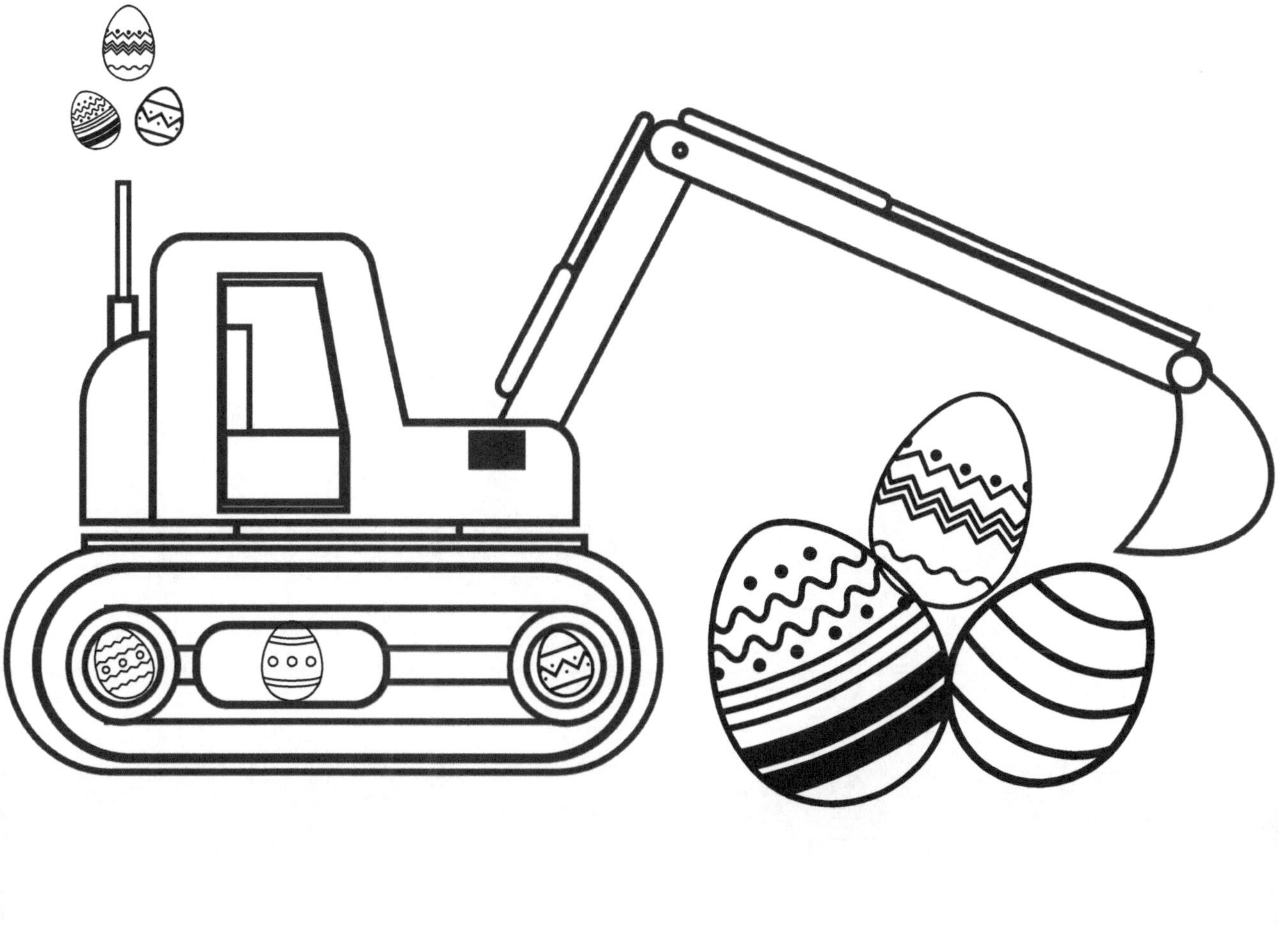

I DIG EASTER

Made in United States
Troutdale, OR
04/17/2025